A 30 Day Guide to Healing

Loss of Your Pet

Gael J. Ross

Licensed Clinical Social Worker

Broken Heart Press

Chapel Hill, North Carolina

For information contact

Gael J. Ross at gjross08@gmail.com
http://petlossguide.net

Published in Chapel Hill, North Carolina by Broken Heart Press
108 Village Crossing Drive, Chapel Hill, NC 27517

Library of Congress Catalog Card Number: 2010910707
ISBN: 978-0-615-38298-2

If you would like, you can paste a picture of your pet on this page.

The purpose of this book is to provide a resource to help animal owners work through the pain following the loss of their pet. In our society, there is often a message that there must be something wrong with anyone who feels despair or "falls apart" over the loss of an animal. Because of this message, the "survivors" of animal loss are often left feeling alone and "crazy" because they are having such a strong reaction to their loss. As a psychotherapist of many years helping clients cope with a number of issues, I have frequently been told in the utmost confidence that "I felt worse about the loss of my dog than I did about the death of a family member." When these words were uttered, it was almost always with a sense of shame and guilt.

In the past few years, it has been recognized that the feeling of loss experienced when a beloved pet dies can be as intense as, or even greater than, that experienced when a human acquaintance dies. With this recognition, thankfully, those suffering from the loss of an animal companion no longer need to hide their grief or feel shame as they continue to mourn. In addition, a number of helpful and supportive resources for dealing with these feelings are now available. At the end of this guide I have provided a selected list of these resources. Some are other publications while several are telephone contacts or web sites.

It is my hope that this book will offer some help to all those who are mourning, have mourned, or will be mourning the loss of their animal companion(s). I have lost and mourned many animals in my lifetime, and I know from first hand experience how painful this loss can be. I also know from having attended as a "survivor" as well as having organized my own grief groups how helpful it is to know you are not alone. I think the recognition of the legitimacy of the devastating feelings surrounding animal loss is very important. Experts agree that the loss of a child is one of life's most traumatic events. For many animal owners, their pets **are** their children. Fortunately, there are now many counselors who work in the area of pet loss providing both individual and group bereavement counseling. This book is not, nor is it meant to be, a substitute for these types of counseling. Rather, it is intended as an aid and supplement based on my own personal and professional experiences in dealing with the death of a beloved pet. Ultimately, everyone mourns at a different pace, and so consider this book a guide, and not the final word.

DEDICATION

This book is dedicated to Madison, who adorns the cover of the book. He was my best friend, travel companion, both on the highway and all of life's other journeys. With his loss, I lost a piece of myself and especially a piece of my heart.

The book is also dedicated to all my past pets: One cat named "The Cat" and several dogs including Cookie, Poncho, Laddie, Pugsley, Mrs. Jones, and JP Snooze, who was with me for almost 18 years. And, of course, it is also dedicated to all pet owners around the world who know both the joys of animal companionship as well as the pain of losing that companion.

Surviving The Loss of Your Pet

THE SEVEN R'S to RECOVERY

Reacting With Shock

Recrimination

Rumination

Reaching Out

Reliving - Regretting

Resolving - Readjusting

Rallying - Recovering

REACTING WITH SHOCK AND DISBELIEF

This is usually the first reaction that you have when you learn that your pet has been severely injured or has a terminal illness. It is also the same reaction that you have upon the actual death of your pet. Often, the more sudden the death, the stronger the reaction. With some severe reactions, the pet owner might even lapse into denial of the actual loss.

RECRIMINATION

This is the period of time when you might feel angry at both yourself and others. You might be beating yourself up for a variety of reasons. These could include letting your pet off leash, forgetting to give medications, not getting to the veterinarian sooner and, most common of all, not having recognized early symptoms. Understandably, you might also be directing your anger and frustration at your veterinarian.

RUMINATION

Rumination is the stage where one goes over and over previous events, searching for alternatives that might have saved your pet's life. It is an endless cycle of "would have, could have, should have." Some people are more prone to rumination than others, and for those who are engaged in this kind of thinking, it brings about extreme sadness and depression. It is a form of obsessing that does nothing other than make one feel worse than one already does.

REACHING OUT - MOVING FORWARDS

This is the phase where it might be helpful for you to talk to other people who can understand your loss. Make sure that you choose those who can understand the pain you feel at losing your animal friend. You don't want to share with people who lack an understanding of how important a pet can be. It is the time you might consider finding a support group of others who have lost a pet.

RELIVING-REGRETTING - GOING BACKWARDS

This is the phase where you start rethinking the things that you wish you had done differently. It is really going back to the "ruminating" phase where you are blaming yourself for everything that brought about the death of your pet. Such thoughts feed a fantasy (however futile) that something you might have done could have saved your pet's life. It is normal for such self-blame to occur. Remember, grief is often two steps forward and one step back. The sooner you can stop this backwards movement the better.

RESOLVING - READJUSTING

It is at this point that you begin to stop blaming yourself and others and recognize that no one is perfect. Rather than thinking only with your heart, you are starting to think with your head as well. You will still be feeling pain, but it is less intense and less omnipresent.

RALLYING - RECOVERING

In the beginning, recovery from your loss may feel impossible. You are now feeling more energy and are able to take on more real world tasks. You might take up activities that you did not pursue when you were so absorbed by your pet's illness and subsequent death. You might go on trips that you did not want to take for fear of leaving your pet. You might change your appearance, move, or engage in just about any activity that leads to making a life for yourself without your beloved pet by your side.

Day One -The Beginning of Your Journal

Day One

Beginning today it might be helpful to keep a diary of how you are feeling. The pages on the left side of the book have been set aside to keep such a journal. Try to recognize where you are in the 7 R's of recovery. Please remember that your feelings will probably change from day to day. They might even change from hour to hour. There is no way around the pain of loss, but there is a way through it.

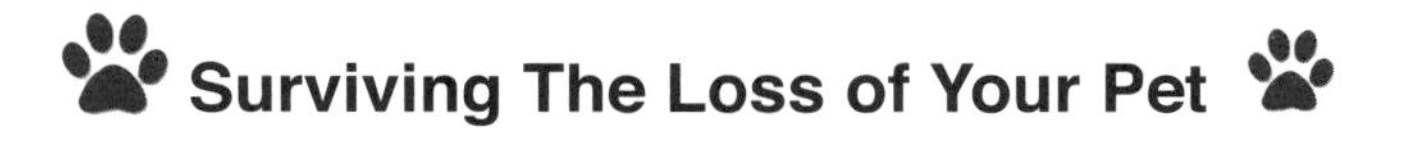
Surviving The Loss of Your Pet

Day Two

Day Two

There is never a good time to say goodbye.

All of life involves losing the ones we love

unless, of course, we go first.

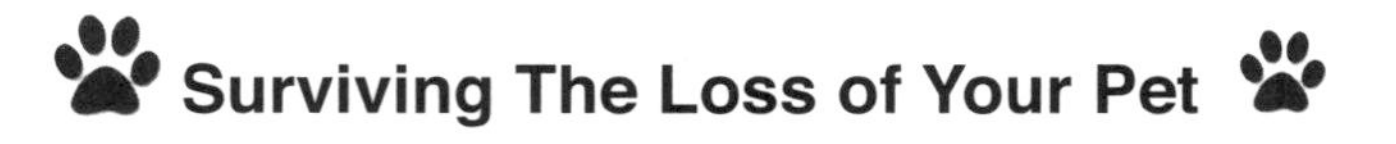
Surviving The Loss of Your Pet

Day Three

Day Three

Don't cry because it's over.

Smile because it happened.

Ted Geisel (Dr. Seuss)

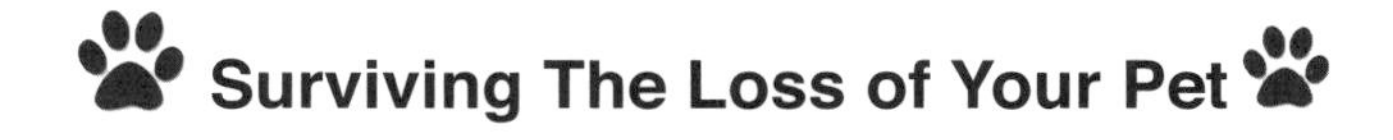
Surviving The Loss of Your Pet

Day Four

Day Four

In the end, you have little or no control over your pet's death. You may be going over "would have, could have, should have," but you made the best decision you could with the information you had. This pertains, particularly, if you had to choose euthanasia.

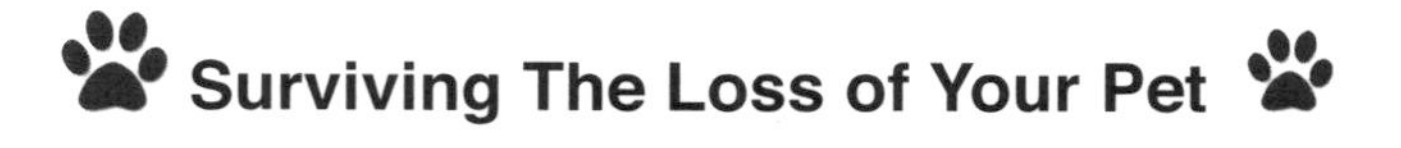
Surviving The Loss of Your Pet

Day Five

Day Five

You did everything to give your pet a good life, and there is no doubt that you did. Your pet knew that you loved him and only did what was best for him. Try not to think of how you could have done things differently.

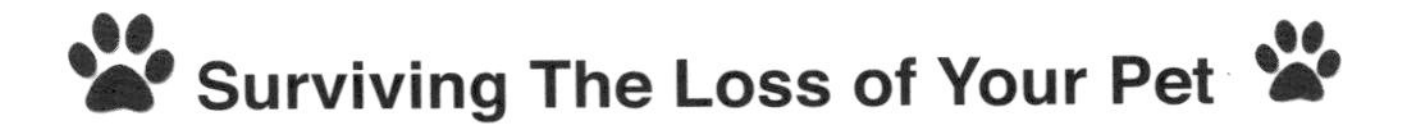
Surviving The Loss of Your Pet

Day Six

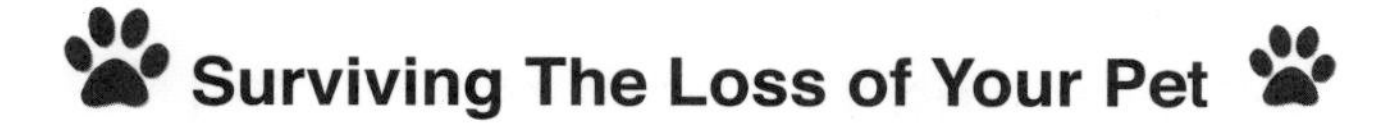

Day Six

Don't blame yourself. It is normal, but it will only make you feel worse. It is hard enough losing your best friend, so don't make it more difficult than it already is. Sometimes we just have to accept that we are not perfect. Ah, if only that were not the case.

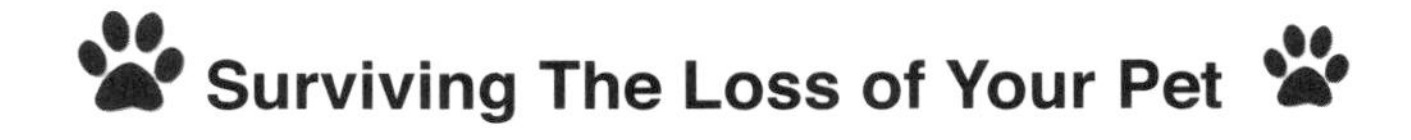
Surviving The Loss of Your Pet

Day Seven

Day Seven

For those who love their pets, it would be the worst form of a lie to call any place where they were banned "Paradise." Certainly no loving God would separate people from their animal friends for eternity.

Stanley Coren, dog psychologist

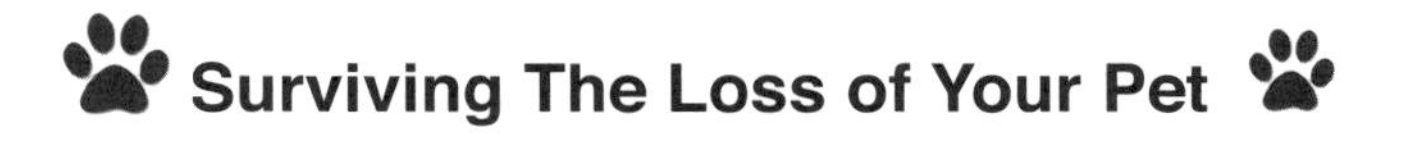
Surviving The Loss of Your Pet

Day Eight

Day Eight

Think of one funny thing your pet did on a regular basis that made you laugh and try to laugh today just thinking about it. You could even think of several funny things your pet did and try to laugh at each of them one by one.

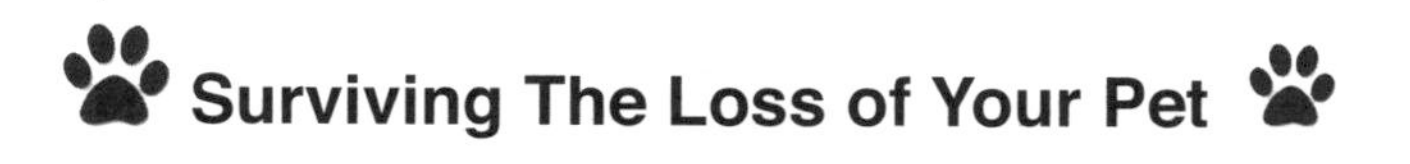
Surviving The Loss of Your Pet

Day Nine

Day Nine

Remember, beginnings are wonderful, and endings are very painful. But, you can have no beginnings without endings and no endings without beginnings.

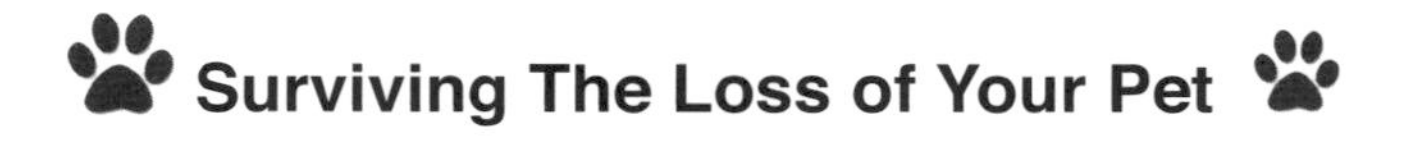
Surviving The Loss of Your Pet

Day Ten

Day Ten

Not the least hard thing to bear when they go from us, these quiet friends, is that they carry away with them so many years of our own lives.

John Galsworthy

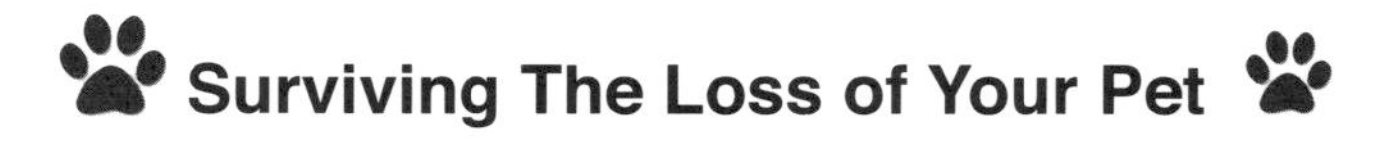
Surviving The Loss of Your Pet

Day Eleven

Day Eleven

There are only two ways to relieve the pain of loss.

One is time, and the other is what you tell yourself.

You do have control over what you tell yourself.

So, tell yourself the things that will make you feel better rather than what makes you feel worse.

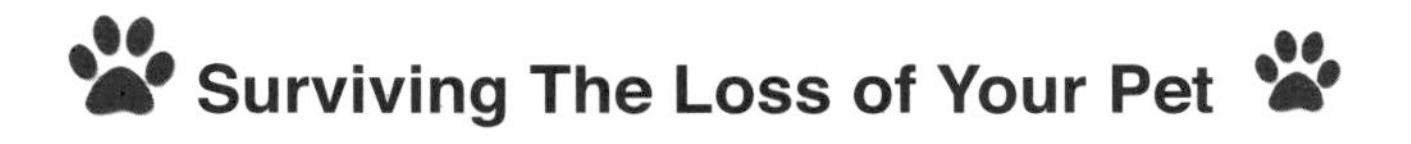
Surviving The Loss of Your Pet

Day Twelve

Day Twelve

If you had to make the decision to euthanize your pet, you had to make a difficult and painful decision. But remember, you made this decision to stop your pet's pain and agony and allow your pet to die without unnecessary suffering.

Day Thirteen

Day Thirteen

If you have a dog, you will most likely outlive it; to get a dog is to open yourself to profound joy and, prospectively, to equally profound sadness.

Marjorie Garber, English Professor, Harvard University

Day Fourteen

Day Fourteen

No matter how long we have had our pet, there is never the right time to "let go" of them. And, there is no letting go without pain. Sadly enough, this time always comes too soon. We know all of this in our heads, but in our hearts it is another matter.

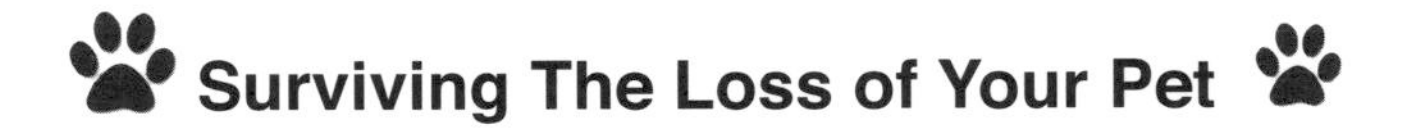
Surviving The Loss of Your Pet

Day Fifteen

Day Fifteen

Remember, death ends a life, not a relationship.

Jack Lemmon

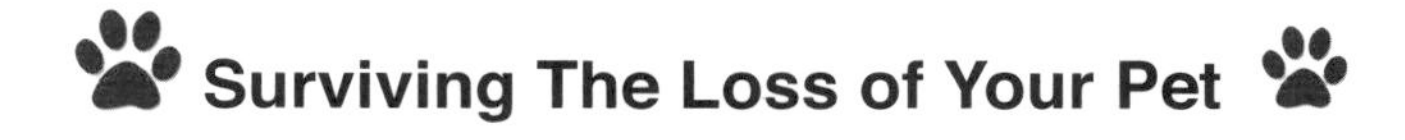
Surviving The Loss of Your Pet

Day Sixteen

Day Sixteen

The risk of love is loss, and the price of loss is grief.

But the pain of grief is only a shadow when compared with the pain of never risking love.

Hillary Stanton Zunin

Day Seventeen

Day Seventeen

Don't blame yourself or anyone else.

It won't change anything!

And it won't bring back your pet.

Day Eighteen

Day Eighteen

Each day you will start feeling better, or at least a little less devastated by your loss. Are you feeling better today than you were two weeks ago? Are you able not to get tears in your eyes when someone says, "I am so sorry for your loss?"

Day Nineteen

Day Nineteen

If you still feel very sad, that is normal. If you still feel very very sad, that is also normal. However, if you still feel overwhelmingly sad, maybe this would be a good time to join a pet loss support group. Sometimes only one session can help you gain perspective. In some situations it might take a few. In any case, it can be very helpful to be around others who understand and are feeling the same pain.

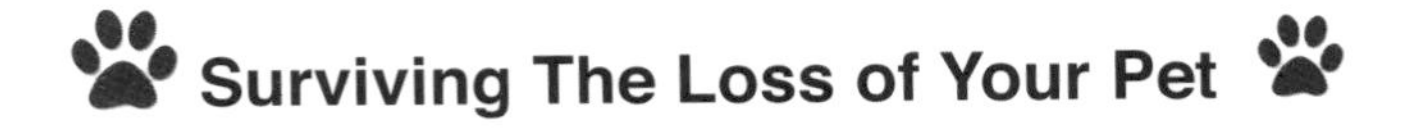
Surviving The Loss of Your Pet

Day Twenty

Day Twenty

Read Rainbow Bridge*

Even if you don't believe in heaven and hell, you might start believing in heaven. What do you have to lose?

*A copy of Rainbow Bridge is at the end of this book.

Day Twenty-One

Day Twenty-One

Maybe it is time to start thinking about getting a new friend? Maybe it is not? That is a very individual decision and should be made by **you** alone. You might even want to visit your local animal shelters where millions of pets are just waiting for a wonderful owner such as yourself. Or, if you are not ready for a permanent new companion, you might even think of becoming a foster parent for animals requiring temporary living quarters. Some of your local shelters or rescue groups can give you information on fostering which is so badly needed.

Day Twenty-Two

Day Twenty-Two

Your old friend, who is now in dog or cat heaven, is saying they understand if you feel guilty when you think of *replacing* them. But both you and your pet know it is not replacing that you are trying to do. Rather, it should be thought of as ***tribute*** to your old companion.
Your animal buddy has been such a rewarding friend, and you know that you want another chance to repeat that kind of relationship with another animal.

Day Twenty-Three

Day Twenty-Three

Moving forward means being able to open up to new friends as well as future losses. But, at this point try to focus on the joy of the new rather than the sorrow of the loss. Life is what you choose to focus on, so try to focus on the positive and not the negative.

Day Twenty-Four

Day Twenty-Four

Grief is like the ocean; it comes in waves ebbing and flowing. Sometimes the water is calm, and sometimes it is overwhelming. All we can do is learn to swim.

Vicki Harrison

Day Twenty-Five

Day-Twenty-Five

I have sometimes thought of the final cause of dogs having such short lives and I am quite satisfied it is in compassion to the human race; for if we suffer so much in losing a dog after an acquaintance of ten or twelve years, what would it be if they were to live double that time?

Sir Walter Scott

Day Twenty-Six

Day Twenty-Six

It may be that the most profound benefit of having a pet is that we come to understand better the experience of death, and, perhaps, lose some of our fear of it in the process.....Death, our pets teach us, is necessary for new life to appear, both for our pets and eventually, for us too.

Martin Goldstein, DVM,
"The Nature of Animal Healing"

Day Twenty-Seven

Day Twenty-Seven

You can't see anything properly while

your eyes are blurred with tears.

C.S. Lewis

Day Twenty-Eight

Day Twenty-Eight

I wanted a perfect ending. Now I've learned, the hard way, that some poems don't rhyme, and some stories don't have a clear beginning, middle, and end. Life is about not knowing, having to change, taking the moment and making the best of it, without knowing what's going to happen next.

Gilda Radner

Day Twenty-Nine

Day Twenty-Nine

You might be feeling very alone in your sadness, but know that anyone who has ever lost a pet they were very attached to knows your pain.

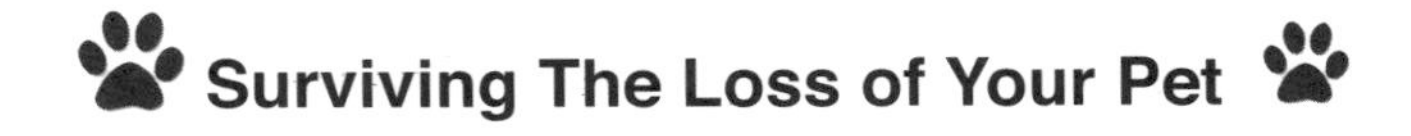
Surviving The Loss of Your Pet

Day Thirty

Day Thirty

People search their entire lives for unconditional love, and we find it in our pets. It is often the most perfect relationship that we have. Unlike so many "human" relationships, our relationships with our pets are free of all the complications and emotional baggage that so often accompany the human-human bond. No wonder saying goodbye is so hard to do.

Jeanine Wordley, DVM, LCSW

Day Thirty-One
Where Am I Now?

Day Thirty-One

Where Am I Now?

Still in shock?

or

Recrimination

Rumination

Reaching Out - Moving Forwards

Reliving-Regretting - Moving Backwards

Resolving - Readjusting

Rallying - Recovering

What is Loss?

Loss is an ending or a point of **change**.

TYPES OF LOSS ESPECIALLY RELATED TO PET LOSS

The **actual loss** of your pet

The **VOID** in your life created by the pet's absence

The **cause not certain** or the **pet disappears**

The loss is **associated with earlier losses**

Surviving The Loss of Your Pet

Losses that can have the greatest impact on pet owners are those in which the pet played a significant role in their daily life. The loss of such a pet can create a major feeling of total emptiness with a struggle to create a new and different routine.

Surviving The Loss of Your Pet

Four Tasks Necessary to Complete Mourning*

1. The first is to accept the reality of the loss, that reunion is impossible, at least in this life.
2. Second, to work through the pain of the grief.
3. Third, to adjust to an environment in which the deceased is missing.
4. Finally, to emotionally relocate the deceased and move on with life.

* J. William Worden, Grief Counseling & Grief Therapy

Task One - Acceptance

The opposite of acceptance is denial. **Denial** can occur in several forms and can manifest itself in three different ways.

Denial of the loss

Denial of the meaning of the loss

Denial of the irreversality of the loss

Task Two - Pain

The second task is to work through the pain of the grief. If we do not experience the pain of loss, it means that we probably could not FEEL the joy of the days we had with our beloved pet. Unfortunately, feelings come in all different forms. They consist of both pain and pleasure. You can't have one without the other. Because the pain from the loss of a pet is frequently not recognized by society, it can result in the griever denying the pain to both himself and others. This is not good as the pain needs to be acknowledged in order to work through the other three tasks of mourning.

Task Three

The third task is adjusting to a life without your pet. This can be especially difficult for people whose pet was an integral part of their daily life. I think for many pet owners, single or coupled, there are daily habits that we have with our pets. The involuntary change in those habits can be over-whelming. Pets give us a sense of structure and continuity. When our pet is gone so is the established pattern of our daily life.

Task Four

To emotionally relocate your pet in your heart and in your mind, and move forward in your life.
For some of us this can take longer than others, but it is a most necessary step. Until we come to terms with our loss, the road forward will be very difficult. Of course, there may be many bumps along the way, but forward we must go!!

I feel about my dogs now, and all the dogs I had prior to this, the way I feel about children - they are that important to me. When I have lost a dog I have gone into a mourning period that lasted for months.

Mary Tyler Moore

Surviving The Loss of Your Pet

*I*t came to me that every time I lose a pet they take a piece of my heart with them.

And every new pet who comes into my life gifts me with a piece of their heart.

If I live long enough, all the components of my heart will be a dog or cat, and I will become as generous and loving as they are.

Anonymous

Rainbow Bridge

Just this side of heaven is a place called Rainbow
Bridge.
When an animal dies that has been especially close t
someone here, that pet goes to Rainbow Bridge.
There are meadows and hills for all of our specia
friends so they can run and play together.
There is plenty of food, water and sunshine, and ou
friends are warm and comfortable.
All the animals who had been ill and old are restored t
health and vigor; those who were hurt or maimed ar
made whole and strong again, just as we remembe
them in our dreams of days and times gone by.
The animals are happy and content, except for on

mall thing; they each miss someone very special to hem, who had to be left behind.

hey all run and play together, but the day comes when ne suddenly stops and looks into the distance. His right eyes are intent; His eager body quivers. uddenly he begins to run from the group, flying over he green grass, his legs carrying him faster and aster.

ou have been spotted, and when you and your special riend finally meet, you cling together in joyous reunion, ever to be parted again. The happy kisses rain upon our face; your hands again caress the beloved head, nd you look once more into the trusting eyes of your et, so long gone from your life but never absent from our heart.

Only people who are capable of loving strongly can also suffer great sorrow, but this same necessity of loving serves to counteract their grief and heals them.

Tolstoy

Resources for Pet Bereavement Counseling

Hotlines and Counseling Centers

Arizona
Companion Animal Association of Arizona
Scottsdale 602 - 995-5885

California
The Grief Recovery Institute
Beverly Hills 888 - 773-2683

University of California School of Veterinary Medicine
Davis 530 - 752-4200

Surviving The Loss of Your Pet

Colorado

Colorado State University School of Veterinary Medicine
Fort Collins 970 - 491-1242

Florida

University of Florida School of Veterinary Medicine
Gainesville 352 - 392 - 4700, Extension 4080

Illinois

C.A.R.E. Pet Loss Helpline, University of Illinois
Urbana 217- 244-2273 or 877- 394-2273
Chicago Veterinary Medical Association
Chicago 630- 325-1600

Surviving The Loss of Your Pet

Iowa

Iowa State University School of Veterinary Medicine
Ames 888 - 478-7574

Massachusetts

Tufts University School of Veterinary Medicine
Grafton 508 - 839-7966

Michigan

Michigan State University School of Veterinary Medicine
Lansing 517 - 432-2696

Surviving The Loss of Your Pet

Minnesota

The Broken Bond Pet Loss Hotline/Support Group
Rochester 507 - 289-8169

University of Minnesota School of Veterinary Medicine
St. Paul 612 - 625-1919

Animal Humane Society of Hennepin County
Minneapolis 952 - 522-6009

New Jersey

Pet Friends, Inc.
Moorsetown 800 - 404-7387

St. Hubert's Giralda
Madison 973 - 377-7094

Surviving The Loss of Your Pet

New York

Animal Medical Center
New York City 212 - 838-8100

ASPCA
New York City 212 - 876-7700

Bide-A-Wee Foundation
New York City 212 - 532-6395

Capitol Region Pet Loss Network
Albany 518 - 448-5677

Cornell University
Ithaca 607 - 253-3932

Surviving The Loss of Your Pet

Ohio

Ohio State University

Columbus 614 - 292-1823

Pennsylvania

University of Pennsylvania School of Veterinary Medicine

Philadelphia 215 - 898-4525

Tennessee

Veterinary Social Work

PAUSEline 865 - 755-8839

Virginia

Virginia-Maryland College of Veterinary Medicine

Blacksburg 540 - 231-8038

Washington
Washington State University College of Veterinary Medicine
Pet Loss Hotline
Pullman 509 - 335-5704
e-mail: plhl@vetmed.wsu.edu
www.vetmed.wsu.edu/plhl

Wisconsin
The Rainbow Passage, Pet Loss Support and Bereavement Center
Grafton 414 - 376-0340
e-mail: douglasc@execpc.com

Surviving The Loss of Your Pet

The Delta Society

Bellevue, Washington
206-226-7357
email: info@deltasociety.org

The Delta Society is a non-profit organization with focus on the human animal bond.
They have created an easy-to-use directory of resources to aid you throughout your grieving process. In addition to the non-profit groups previously listed, they have a list of private therapists who specialize in the grief following the loss of a pet.

Bibliography

rviving the Heartbreak of Choosing Death for Your Pet, Linda Peterson. West Chester, PA: Greentree Publishing, 1997. 153 pages.

'hen Your Pet Dies: How to Cope With Your Feelings, Jamie Quackenbush. New York: Pocket Books, 1985. 223 pages.

'ieving the Death of a Pet, Betty J. Carmack. Minneapolis, MN: Augsburg Fortress, 2003. 119 pages.

ɔw to Go On Living When Someone You Love Dies, Therese A. Rando, Ph.D., Lexington, MA: Lexington Books, 1988. 338 pages.

e Loss of A Pet, A Guide to Coping with the Grieving Process When A Pet Dies, Wallace Sife, Ph.D, Hobeken, NJ: Howell Book House, 2005. 260 pages.

Grief Counseling and Grief Therapy: A Handbook for the Mental Health Practitioner, J. William Worden. New York: Springer Publishing Company, 1991. 183 pages.

Goodbye, friend, Gary Kowalski, Walpole. New Hampshire: Stillpoint Publishing, 1997. 159 pages.

Journey Through Pet Loss, Deborah Antinori. Basking Ridge, NJ: YokoSpirit Publications, 2000, Audio, 3 hours. 8 minutes.